I See Nu...

By Pamela Chanko

ISBN: 978-1-338-88852-2

Editor: Liza Charlesworth
Art Director: Tannaz Fassihi; Designer: Tanya Chernyak
Photos ©: 4: clu/Getty Images; 7: Mouse in the House/Alamy Stock Photo;
8: dubassy/Getty Images. All other photos © Shutterstock.com.

1 2 3 4 5 6 7 8 9 10   68   31 30 29 28 27 26 25 24 23
Printed in Jiaxing, China. First printing, January 2023.

SCHOLASTIC INC.

I see numbers on a train.

I see numbers on a game.

I see numbers on a clock.

I see numbers on a door.

I see numbers on a shirt.

I see numbers on a phone.

I see numbers in my soup!